Science Experiment

WITH

COLOUR

Sally Nankivell-Aston
and Dorothy Jackson

W

FRANKLIN WATTS
LONDON•SYDNEY

This edition 2003

Franklin Watts
96 Leonard Street, London EC2A 4XD

Franklin Watts Australia
45-51 Huntley Street
Alexandria
NSW 2015

Series editor: Rachel Cooke
Designer: Mo Choy
Picture research: Susan Mennell
Photography: Ray Moller, unless otherwise
acknowledged

A CIP catalogue record for this book
is available from the British Library.

ISBN 0 7496 5341 8

Dewey Classification 537

Printed in Malaysia

Acknowledgements:
Cover: Steve Shott; AKG Photos, London p. 6br
(Musée Condé, Chantilly); Bruce Coleman pp. 4b
(Christer Fredriksson), 5bl (Jules Cowan), 14t (Joe
McDonald); Image Bank pp. 9bl (Jeff Spielman), 9br
(Andy Caulfield); Oxford Scientific Films pp.4m
(Alistair Shay), 5tr, 5br (Robin Redfern), 12b (Zig
Leszczynski), 29tr (Michael Fogden), 29b (Wendy
Shattil and Bob Rozinski); Panos Pictures pp.17m (Ray
Wood), 25tr (James Bedding); Science Photo Library
pp. 4t (John Mead), 10b (Vaughan Fleming), 19t (Jerry
Mason), 27t (Jon Wilson).

Thanks, too, to our models: Erin Bhogal, Perry
Christian, Bonita Crawley, Jaimé Leigh Pyle, Jordan
Oldfield, Nicholas Payne, Jennifer Quaife and
Alexander Smale.

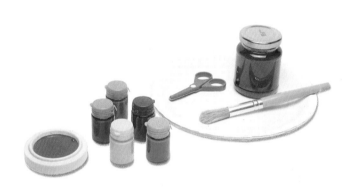

Contents

Colour all around

LOOK AROUND YOU WHEREVER you are and you see colours. Colours can be bright or dull, 'warm' or 'cold', blend together or contrast, they may be natural or made artificially. Look at the pictures and see how many shades of the same colour you can spot.

What is your favourite colour? Is it the same colour that your friend likes best? Discover all about your favourite colours as you do the experiments in this book.

Be amazed!

By doing the experiments in this book you can find out some amazing things about colour. You will find out about the colours of paint and light, how we see colours and how colours can be useful to us, other animals and plants. Some experiments may answer questions that you already ask about colour. Some may make you think of more!

Look closely!

Scientists always ask lots of questions and observe carefully. When you are doing experiments in this book, look closely to see what is happening and keep accurate records of your results. Don't be upset if your predictions do not always turn out to be correct as scientists (and that includes you) learn a lot from unexpected results.

Be careful!

Always make sure an adult knows that you are doing an experiment. Ask for help if you need to use sharp tools, heat things or use chemicals. Follow the step-by-step instructions carefully and remember – be a safe scientist!

Mixing paints

HAVE YOU EVER NOTICED how many different colours of paint you can buy? Each paint contains a natural or artificial pigment to give it colour. All colour pigments are actually made by mixing only two or more of three colours: red, yellow and blue. These are the primary colours of pigments. Find out more in this first experiment.

1 Put a small pool of paint on each saucer – one colour onto each. The paint must be runny so add water if necessary and mix in with a paintbrush. Use a separate paintbrush for each colour.

2 Use the paintbrushes to scatter drops of the three colours, each colour on a separate piece of paper. Then put drops of a second colour as shown. Don't let the drops touch each other!

In action

Today most paint pigments are made from artificial ingredients. However they used to be made from natural materials like plants, rocks and dead insects. The pigment for the blue paint in this 15th-century picture was made by crushing the semiprecious stone, lapis lazuli.

3 Use the straw to blow the paint across the paper so that the colours mix.

4 What happens when red and yellow mix? What happens when red and blue mix? What happens when yellow and blue mix? The mixed colours are called secondary colours. Put your answers on a table like the one below.

Keep thinking

How would you make a paint lighter? How could you make paint darker? How could you get different shades of green?

PRIMARY COLOURS MIXED	SECONDARY COLOUR MADE
red and yellow	
yellow and blue	
red and blue	

5 Now find out what colour you get if all three primary colours are mixed together. This is called a tertiary colour.

Don't stop there

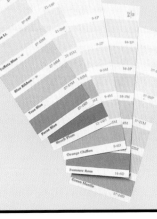

● Drop oil-based inks (marbling inks) onto water in a tray. Swirl the colours around with a cocktail stick. What colours do you get? 'Capture' the colours by gently lowering a piece of paper on top of the water and then removing it carefully.

● Go to a DIY store and get some paint charts. How many different types of blue are there? How many different types of red are there?

Mixing light

ALTHOUGH LIGHT USUALLY looks white it is really made up of different colours. The primary colours of light are red, green and blue. They are not exactly the same as those in pigments and they don't mix in the same way. Find out how these colours of light mix in this experiment.

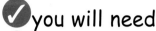
you will need
✓ 3 torches with strong beams
✓ 3 colour filters (red, green and blue)
✓ 3 kitchen roll cardboard tubes
✓ sticky tape
✓ 2 friends

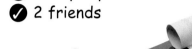

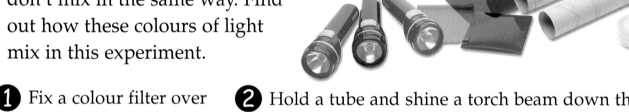

1 Fix a colour filter over the end of each cardboard tube with tape.

2 Hold a tube and shine a torch beam down the open end onto a pale coloured wall in a dark room. Ask your friends to do the same with the other two tubes. Can you see each colour on the wall?

Keep thinking

Look back to pages 6/7 to find out which of the primary colours of light are the same as the primary colours of pigments.

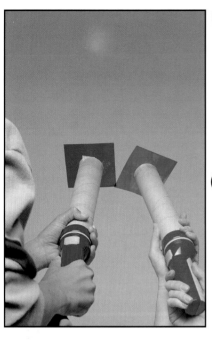

3 What colour do you predict you will see when the red and green lights are mixed together? Find out by making the two colours of light overlap on the wall.

4 In the same way find out what happens when red and blue lights mix, then green and blue? The resulting colours are called the secondary colours of light.

PRIMARY COLOURS MIXED	SECONDARY COLOUR MADE
red and green	
red and blue	
green and blue	

5 Record your results on a table like this one.

Don't stop there

● Find out what colour you get when all three are mixed together.

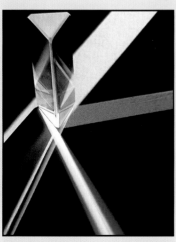

● You can split white light into its different colours using a prism. Shine a strong torch beam through a prism placed on a light piece of paper. What colours can you see on the paper?

In action

Dramatic lighting effects are achieved by mixing different coloured spotlights in theatres, at pop concerts or even on a dance floor.

Seeing colours

IMAGINE WHAT THE world would look like if you couldn't see any colours! We have special cells called cones in our eyes that let us to see in colour. There are about 7 million cones in each of your eyes!

iris
retina
pupil
lens
cone

This diagram shows the different parts of the eye and a close up of some of its cones, which are found in the retina. Some cones see red, some blue and others green. Find out more in this eye-opening experiment!

✔ you will need
- ✔ coloured paper (red, green and blue)
- ✔ 4 pieces of white A4 card
- ✔ scissors
- ✔ pencil
- ✔ ruler
- ✔ glue

1 Cut out red, green and blue squares, each measuring 10 x 10 cm.

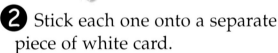

2 Stick each one onto a separate piece of white card.

In action

This is a TV screen close up! Pictures on the screen are made up of tiny dots or stripes of green, red and blue – the primary colours of light. Looked at from a distance, these colours mix and merge to form the multicoloured picture we see.

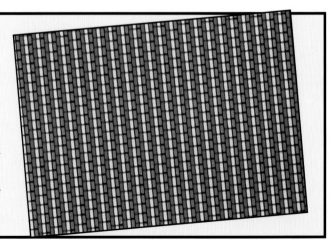

3 Now stare hard at the card with the red square for 30 seconds.

4 Then quickly look at a plain white piece of card. What do you see?

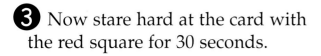
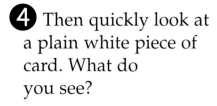

5 Now repeat the experiment in the same way first with the green square, then with the blue.

6 What shape do you see on the white piece of card each time? What colour is it? Add your results to a table like the one below.

COLOUR OF SQUARE	red	green	blue
SHAPE OF IMAGE SEEN ON WHITE CARD			
COLOUR OF IMAGE SEEN ON WHITE CARD			

Keep thinking

As you stared at a coloured square the cones that see that colour got tired so only the cones that see the other two colours were working. How does this explain what you saw when you looked at the plain white card?

Don't stop there

● Repeat the experiment with a yellow square. What colour is the image this time?

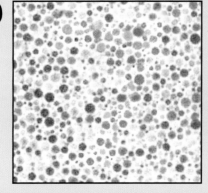

● People who are colour blind cannot see certain colours. Look at this picture. Can you see the number? Some colour-blind people would not be able to read the number picked out in shades of green.

Standing out

COLOURS ARE OFTEN USED to make things stand out and be noticed. For example, cyclists often wear bright colours so motorists can see them easily. Find out which colours stand out best in this experiment.

1 Draw a large exclamation mark on each piece of white card using a different coloured marker pen each time. Make sure they are all about the same size and shape to make the test fair.

2 Predict which colour can be seen from the furthest distance.

Keep thinking

Male birds are often brightly coloured so they can be seen easily. Why do you think they want to be noticed?

In action

Some animals are brightly coloured to warn other animals that they are dangerous or taste disgusting. This tree frog is poisonous. Its colour warns other animals not to eat it.

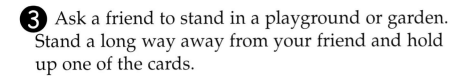

3 Ask a friend to stand in a playground or garden. Stand a long way away from your friend and hold up one of the cards.

4 Gradually walk closer to your friend and ask him/her to say when the exclamation mark can be seen clearly. Measure the distance from your friend to this point.

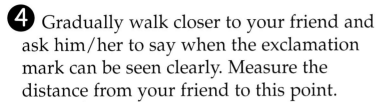

5 Repeat the test with the other colours and record your results in a table like this:

COLOUR OF EXCLAMATION MARK	DISTANCE IT CAN BE SEEN FROM

6 Which colour was easiest to see? Which was most difficult? Which colour would be best to use to write DANGER on a warning sign?

Don't stop there

• Cut out some exclamation marks from white paper (they must be the same size and shape). Stick each one on a different coloured piece of card or paper. Repeat the experiment to see which coloured background makes the white exclamation mark stand out most.

• Look around at signs on the roads and streets. Which colours have been used to make the signs?

Now you see me, now you don't!

ALTHOUGH SOME ANIMALS are brightly coloured to be noticed, others have dull colours to help them hide. They are camouflaged amongst the colours of their natural environment. This means that predators can hunt without being seen and prey animals are less likely to be caught. Find out more about camouflage in this experiment.

In action

Chameleons are camouflage experts! As the colours around them change, their skin colour changes to match.

✔ you will need
- ✔ brown and black felt tip pens
- ✔ 2 hard-boiled hen eggs (brown)
- ✔ a range of natural materials collected from a park or garden
- ✔ different art/craft materials in assorted colours

❶ First add speckles to your eggs with the felt tip pens to make them look like this quail egg.

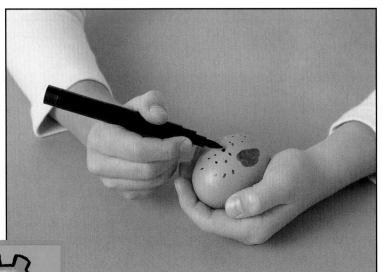

2 Now make two nests, one using the art materials and the other using the natural materials you have collected. Use lots of bright colours for the nest made of art materials but make the natural nest roughly match the colours on the egg.

3 Place an egg in each nest and look at the nests from a short distance.

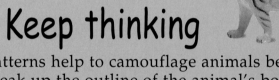

Keep thinking

Patterns help to camouflage animals because they break up the outline of the animal's body. Zebras live on wide grassy plains, tigers in shady jungle. What other animals have patterns to help them hide?

4 Which egg is easiest to see? Why is it easy to see? Which is most difficult? Why? Which nest hides the egg best? Why do you think eggs need to be well hidden?

Don't stop there

● Put the nests in a garden or nature area at school. How long does it take your friends to spot each one? Which is easiest to find? Why?

● Make flower shapes out of different colours of tissue paper. Scatter them around a garden. Which colours are easier to see and which are more difficult?

Hot or cold?

WHY DO PEOPLE OFTEN WEAR white clothes on hot summer days and black clothes during cold winter months? Do you think white clothes make you feel cooler and black clothes make you feel warmer? Find out in this experiment.

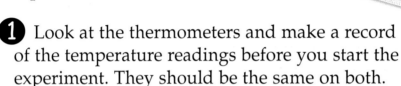

❶ Look at the thermometers and make a record of the temperature readings before you start the experiment. They should be the same on both.

❷ Wrap a small piece of white fur fabric around one of the thermometer bulbs and a black piece around the other. The pieces should be the same size and big enough to wrap around the bulb once. Hold the fabric in place with a small piece of tape.

Keep thinking

What colour clothes do you think would make you feel coolest on a hot day?

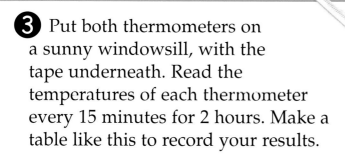

3 Put both thermometers on a sunny windowsill, with the tape underneath. Read the temperatures of each thermometer every 15 minutes for 2 hours. Make a table like this to record your results.

TIME	TEMPERATURE OF WHITE THERMOMETER	TEMPERATURE OF BLACK THERMOMETER
0 mins		
15 mins		
30 mins		
45 mins		
1 hr		
1 hr 15 mins		
1 hr 30 mins		
1 hr 45 mins		
2 hrs		

4 Which thermometer became the hottest? Did the white fabric or the black fabric let the most heat through? Some colours reflect more heat than others, while others absorb heat better. Which fabric reflected the most heat? Do you think white fabrics would keep you cooler on a hot day? Would black fabrics make you feel warmer?

In action

People who live in hot countries often wear light-coloured, loose-fitting clothes to help them keep cool. This man lives in the hot desert regions of Mali in West Africa.

Don't stop there

● Repeat the experiment using different colours of fur fabric or felt. Find out which colours absorb the most heat.

● Put a large piece of fur fabric with a black-and-white design (e.g. imitation cow's skin) in strong sunlight for about half an hour. Stroke your hand over the fabric. Can you feel a difference in temperature between the black and white areas?

A colour detective

A DETECTIVE FOUND A MYSTERIOUS, unsigned note from a criminal. She knew it had been written using one of two black marker pens: one pen belonged to suspect A and one pen belonged to suspect B. The pens were different makes and the detective knew how to find out quickly which suspect had written the note. She used a scientific process called chromatography which separates colours. Here is how the detective solved the case.

you will need
- ✓ 2 black water-soluble marker pens of different makes
- ✓ 2 coffee filter papers
- ✓ 2 drinking beakers
- ✓ dropper (pipette)
- ✓ water in a pot

1 In the centre of each coffee filter paper make a small spot about 1 cm in diameter using one marker pen for each filter. Place a filter paper on top of each beaker.

2 Use the dropper to drop water carefully onto each coloured ink spot. Put the same number of drops on each one to make the test fair.

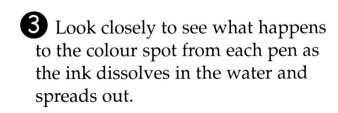

3 Look closely to see what happens to the colour spot from each pen as the ink dissolves in the water and spreads out.

18

In action

Chromatography helps scientists to study diseases, such as cancer. They use it to test tiny samples taken from the human body. There are small differences in the pattern made from a healthy sample and the one made from a sample with the disease.

Keep thinking

Look back to pages 6/7 to find out what colours are made when different coloured paints or pigments are mixed. Did this experiment show the results you expected?

4 Do both ink spots make the same pattern? What colours make up the black colour of each marker? Were you surprised?

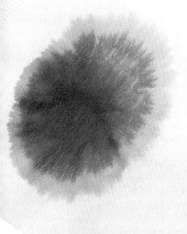

5 How could the detective use the results from this experiment to find out who had written the note?

Don't stop there

• Try repeating the experiment using markers of different colours and find out what colours each one is made from.

• Use chromatography to find out if black writing ink used in fountain pens is made of a mixture of colours. If so are they the same colours as those in black marker pen ink?

Appearing pictures

SOME CHEMICALS CHANGE from transparent to a colour in heat. Amaze your friends with this experiment and make a picture appear 'magically' on plain white paper.

Safety: ask an adult to help you iron the paper in step 3.

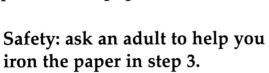
you will need
- ✓ lemon juice in a small pot
- ✓ plain white paper
- ✓ a thin paintbrush
- ✓ a friend!

1 Use the paintbrush to draw a picture with lemon juice on the paper.

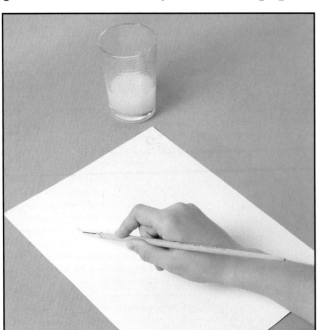

2 Leave the paper to dry so you can hardly see the picture. You have hidden your picture! Show the paper to a friend and ask him or her what they can see on the paper.

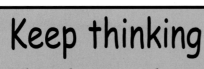
Keep thinking

What other materials can you think of that change colour when they are heated or burnt?

3 Ask an adult to iron over the back of the paper (that is, the side you did not draw on) with a hot iron.

In action

Prisoners used to use saliva or sweat to write secret messages which could be smuggled out to their friends. The messages could only be seen and read when they were heated.

4 Show your friend the paper now. What can be seen? What has changed in the heat to make your picture 'appear'?

Don't stop there

● Do you think other transparent liquids will change in the same way when they are heated? Try the experiment using lemonade and vinegar. What other liquids could you try?
● Ask an adult to light a match. Blow the flame out and look closely at the colour of the wood. How has heat affected the colour of the wood? In what other ways has the wood changed?

Colour tests

YOU CAN USE COLOUR to find out more about the foods we eat and the chemicals we use at home. Some things are acid, some are the opposite, alkaline, and some are neutral, which is in between. Find out more in this experiment.

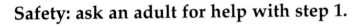

Safety: ask an adult for help with step 1.

1 Chop up some red cabbage leaves and put them into a saucepan with a little water. Heat the pan and boil the cabbage for a few minutes.

2 Let it cool and strain the juice into the bowl. Throw away the cabbage but keep the juice. The juice is for testing the chemicals to find out if they are acid or alkaline. We call it an indicator. What colour is your indicator? It may vary, depending on the type of saucepan you use.

In action

This is universal indicator paper, which scientists use to test for acid and alkaline. Sometimes they test for acid rain which damages plant life, buildings and stone statues.

3 Now add four drops of cabbage water to each saucer containing the kitchen chemicals.

Look closely to see the colour changes of each liquid. Record your results in a table like the one shown.

	COLOUR WHEN CABBAGE WATER IS ADDED	IS IT ACID, ALKALINE OR NEUTRAL?
bicarbonate of soda		
lemon juice		
washing-up liquid		
salt		

4 Red cabbage water is a natural indicator that can be used to tell if substances are acid or alkaline. It turns red in acids and blue/green in alkaline substances. In neutral substances that are neither acid nor alkaline its colour does not change. Can you tell which of your chemicals are acid, alkaline or neutral? Add this to your table.

Don't stop there

● Repeat the experiment to test other foods and common chemicals. You could try milk, orange juice, shower gel and sugar. BE CAREFUL! Ask an adult first in case you want to test something that is harmful. DO NOT use strong or bleach-based cleaning solutions. Record your results in a table.

● Try the experiment again with the water from boiling fresh beetroot (it needs longer cooking than cabbage). What colour changes do you get this time? Are they the same as the colours made with red cabbage water?

Dyeing for colour

WHAT COLOUR IS YOUR favourite shirt or jumper? It was probably dyed using artificial chemicals but how do you think the first dyes were made? Find out how to dye your own fabric using natural colours from everyday things in this experiment.

Safety: ask an adult for help with this experiment.

1 First predict what colour dye each of the different foods will make. Record your ideas in a table like the one shown.

✓ you will need
- ✓ 4 pieces of white cotton fabric, such as handkerchiefs or pieces of an old T-shirt
- ✓ onion skins from at least 2 onions
- ✓ a fresh beetroot chopped into small pieces
- ✓ red cabbage chopped up   ✓ spoon
- ✓ 3 tea bags
- ✓ 4 small bowls
- ✓ elastic bands
- ✓ saucepan
- ✓ sieve

FOOD USED	PREDICTED COLOUR	ACTUAL COLOUR
onion skins		
beetroot		
red cabbage		
tea bag		

2 Prepare the fabrics to be dyed by tying elastic bands tightly at intervals along each piece as shown in the picture.

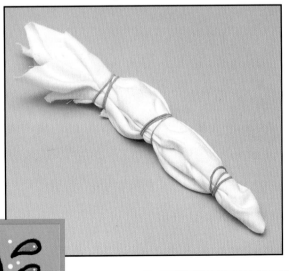

3 Now make your first dye with the onion skins. Put them into the saucepan and pour on enough water to cover them.

Ask an adult to boil up the skins until you can see that the colour from the skins has gone into the water.

4 Use the sieve to strain the coloured liquid into a bowl. This is your dye. Put a piece of fabric into the hot liquid and stir it around with a spoon.

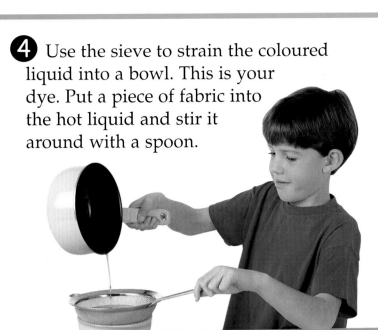

5 Make dyes with the other foods in the same way and put one piece of fabric into each bowl. Leave over night then take out the fabrics and remove the elastic bands.

Keep thinking

Some people make pictures by painting wax onto fabric then dyeing it. Then they iron the fabric between paper to remove the wax. This kind of dyeing is called batik. What effect do you think the wax has?

6 Look closely to see what has happened to the fabric. What colour has the dye from each food turned the fabric? Were your predictions correct? What has happened where the elastic was tied around the fabric? Why?

Don't stop there

● Try to make dye from other foods and plants. You could try petals from brightly coloured flowers, grass, blackberries and coffee. Predict the colour first then make the dyes to find the results.

● Repeat the experiment using different fabrics, such as wool or synthetics, to find out if all cloth absorbs colours from plants in the same way.

Going green!

WHAT COLOUR ARE THE LEAVES of most plants? Do you know why? Plants make their food (a sugar called glucose) using the energy from sunlight, water, carbon dioxide and a green-coloured chemical called chlorophyll. This process is called photosynthesis. Chlorophyll is found mostly in the leaves. Do this experiment and find out more about going green.

✔ **you will need**
- ✔ two similar green-leafed house-plants (NB Don't use a plant with variegated leaves)
- ✔ a dark cupboard
- ✔ labels
- ✔ pen

1 Label the plants A and B. Look closely at the colour of the leaves. Make sure that the plants are well watered.

2 Put plant A into a very dark cupboard – make sure no light can reach it. Put plant B in a light place. Leave both plants for about a week.

In action

Leaves of plants are not always the same shade of green because they contain other pigments as well as chlorophyll. This copper beech still makes its food by photosynthesis but the green chlorophyll is masked by the 'copper' pigments.

3 Take plant A out of the cupboard and place it next to plant B. What do you notice about each plant? Do they still look the same?

4 If the plant has no energy from light it cannot make food and the leaves loose their green colour. What do you think will happen if you put plant B into the cupboard and leave plant A in the light? Test to find out.

5 Leave the plants for the same time as before and then compare them again. What do you notice now? Why do you think the plants have changed?

Keep thinking

In autumn, the leaves on many trees change colour when they die and fall off the tree. Why do you think the leaves lose their green colour?

Don't stop there

Get a plant that has red or patterned leaves. What do you think will happen this time if you repeat the experiment? Test to find out.

Fabulous flowers

Wʜᴀᴛ ɪs ʏᴏᴜʀ ғᴀᴠᴏᴜʀɪᴛᴇ colour? Do you think insects have favourite colours, too? Find out about why flowers have such fabulous colours in this experiment.

Note: it is better to do this experiment in spring or summer when there are plenty of insects around.

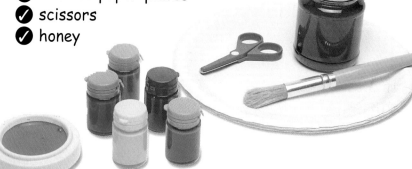

✓ **you will need**
- ✓ red, blue, green, yellow, purple and orange paint
- ✓ 7 white paper plates
- ✓ scissors
- ✓ honey

1 First turn the paper plates into 'flowers'. Cut petal shapes from around the edge as shown and paint each plate a different colour. Leave one white.

2 Put a teaspoon of honey in the centre of each plate. Place the plates in open spaces around a garden or playground on a sunny day.

Keep thinking

Look back to pages 12 and 13 to find out which colour was easiest to see when you made your signs. Is this the same colour as the flower that attracted the most insects in this experiment?

3 Watch carefully for half an hour to see how many insects and other small creatures visit each flower.

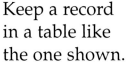

Keep a record in a table like the one shown.

FLOWER COLOUR	NUMBER OF INSECTS VISITING
white	
red	
blue	
yellow	
green	
purple	
orange	

In action

Like many insects, this hummingbird is attracted to brightly coloured flowers and feeds from the sugary nectar inside them. Some pollen from the flowers sticks to the hummingbird and is taken to the next flower it visits. This flower is now able to form seeds, so new plants can grow. This process is called pollination.

4 Which colour flower do the insects visit most? Have you seen lots of real flowers of this colour? Why is it useful to flowers if insects visit them? Which colour do insects visit least? Do you see many flowers of this colour? If not, why not?

Don't stop there

● In an area of wild flowers find out the most common flower colour. Is it the same colour that you found insects visited most?

● Repeat the experiment, but this time keep a record of the type of insects that visit the flowers as well. Do different types of insect prefer different colours?

Glossary

This glossary gives the meaning of each word as it is used in this book.

Acid A chemical that is acid turns indicators red.

Acid rain Acidic pollution from factories and car exhausts carried in the air can dissolve in the water held in clouds. This water then falls as acid rain.

Alkaline A chemical that is alkaline turns indicators blue/green.

Batik A method of producing patterned fabrics using wax to stop dye(s) colouring parts of the fabric.

Camouflage Colourings or patterns to make an animal, person, vehicle or another object difficult to see in its surroundings.

Carbon dioxide A gas in the air that plants use to make food in the process of photosynthesis.

Cell Very small parts of all living things. Cells are sometimes called the building blocks of life.

Chlorophyll The green chemical in plants, that enables them to make food using energy from sunlight, carbon dioxide from the air and water from the ground in a process called photosynthesis.

Chromatography A technique used to separate a mixture of different chemicals, such as pigments, into its different parts.

Colour blind People who are colour blind are unable to see certain colours.

Colour filter A transparent piece of coloured material that allows only light of that colour to pass through it.

Cones Cells in the retina of the eye that enable us to see things in colour.

Diameter The straight line from one edge of a circle to the other passing through its centre.

Dye To dye something is to change its colour by soaking it in a specially coloured liquid. The liquid is also called a dye.

Energy People, plants and animals need energy to live. Machines need energy to work. Energy comes from lots of different sources. Burning petrol gives a car its energy. Food gives us our energy.

Experiment A fair test done to find out more about something or to answer a question. Sometimes called an investigation.

Fair test A scientific test to find an accurate result. To keep the test fair, when you are experimenting, only one part (variable) must be changed and all the other parts (variables) must stay the same.

Filter paper Absorbent paper with very fine holes in it.

Glucose A type of sugar.

Indicator A substance used to find out, or indicate, if a chemical is acid or alkaline.

Iris The coloured part of the eye that surrounds the pupil.

Lapis lazuli A semiprecious, blue mineral that used to be used to make a bright blue pigment for paints. Today, lapis lazuli is more often used in jewellery.

Lens In an eye, the lens focuses the light that enters through the pupil to form a clear image on the retina.

Nectar A sweet liquid made in the flowers of some plants to attract insects and other animals to visit them to help the process of pollination.

Neutral A chemical that is neutral is neither acid nor alkaline. Pure water is neutral.

Photosynthesis The process by which plants use energy from the sun and chlorophyll to make their food.

Pigment A material used to colour paints, inks or dyes.

Pollen Very small grains from the male part of a flower.

Pollination The process by which pollen is transferred from the male part of a flower to a female part to make seeds from which new plants can grow.

Predators Animals that hunt and eat other animals for food.

Predict To guess what will happen in an experiment before doing it.

Prey Animals that are hunted and eaten by other animals for food.

Primary colours of light The three colours of light, red, green and blue, which can be mixed together to create all other light colours.

Primary colours of pigment The three pigment colours, red, blue and yellow, which can be mixed together to create all other colours.

Prism A solid piece of transparent glass or plastic (often looking like a pyramid) that can be used to split white light into its colours.

Pupil A small hole in the iris that lets light into the eye.

Quail A small, short-tailed bird that is a member of the partridge family.

Result(s) The outcome of an experiment.

Retina The back of the inside of the eye made up of light-sensitive cells.

Saliva The liquid in your mouth that helps you to digest and swallow your food.

Secondary colour The colour made when two primary colours mix.

Temperature How hot or cold something is. Temperature is measured in degrees Celsius or Fahrenheit.

Tertiary colour The colour made when three primary colours mix.

Thermometer An instrument to measure temperature.

Transparent Completely see-through.

Universal indicator paper Paper that contains an indicator so that it changes colour when dipped in something that is acid or alkaline. Litmus paper is also used for this.

Index

WOMEN
AND WAR

WOMEN AND WAR

ANN KRAMER

W

FRANKLIN WATTS

LONDON•SYDNEY

Designer Jason Billin
Editor Sarah Ridley
Art Director Jonathan Hair
Editor-in-Chief John C. Miles
Picture research Diana Morris

© 2005 Franklin Watts

First published in 2005
by Franklin Watts
96 Leonard Street
London EC2A 4XD

Franklin Watts Australia
Level 17/207 Kent Street
Sydney NSW 2000

ISBN 0 7496 6358 8

A CIP catalogue record for this book is
available from the British Library.

Printed in China

Dewey number: 940.53'082'0922

Picture credits
Bettmann/Corbis: 25
Cody Images: cover, 2, 8, 11, 16, 19, 20,
   30, 31
John Hinde Archive/HIP/Topham: 9
Peter Newark's Pictures:
   10, 12 detail © DACS London 2005, 18
Picturepoint/Topham: 7, 15, 23, 28, 32
Picture Post/GettyImages: 27
PRO/HIP Topham: 14

Every attempt has been made to clear copyright.
Should there be any inadvertent omission please
apply to the publisher for rectification.

Note to parents and teachers:
Every effort has been made by the Publishers to
ensure that the websites in this book are suitable
for children, that they are of the highest
educational value, and that they contain no
inappropriate or offensive material. However,
because of the nature of the Internet, it is
impossible to guarantee that the contents of these
sites will not be altered. We strongly advise that
Internet access is supervised by a responsible adult.

CONTENTS

Setting the Scene

World War Two (1939–45) was a total war. It involved not just troops but also civilians. Women played an essential part. For some, life would never be the same again.

Peace and Poppies

Some women and women's organisations campaigned for peace between the wars. They included British feminist Dora Russell (1894–1986), the Women's International League for Peace and Freedom (WILPF) and the Women's Freedom League. In 1933 the Women's Co-operative Guild together with the Peace Pledge Union (PPU) created a white poppy. Like the red poppy, it was worn on 11 November to honour the dead of World War One but it also stood for peace. Some people still wear it today.

❝I held my chin high and kept back the tears at the thought of the slaughter ahead.❞

Female schoolteacher, on hearing British Prime Minister Chamberlain announce the declaration of war on the radio.

Experience of War

Women had been involved in war before; thousands of women rallied to the war effort during World War One (1914–18). In that first global conflict, women took over when men left home to fight. They worked in factories making weapons, drove buses and harvested the land, doing so-called "men's work" for the very first time. They nursed the wounded on the front line. In every way, women challenged the image of what women were supposed to be. Most women also lost men close to them – fathers, brothers, husbands, sons and friends who died in the trenches.

Changing Lives

After 1918, women were expected to give up work and return to the home. Most did. But nothing was quite the same again. Women's lives began to change, particularly in Britain and America. They had proved themselves as citizens and now gained the vote – something they had been demanding since the 1840s. By 1931, there were 15 women Members of Parliament (MPs) in Britain.

Around the world millions of women were in waged work. Most were in low-paid jobs but there were greater opportunities. Women could be civil servants, work in law, and serve on juries. Even so, there was a clear division between what people thought was "men's work" and "women's work". Women were definitely expected to give up work when they married.

Women in the late 1930s had more rights than in 1914 but they were not equal with men. People still thought a woman's place was in the home and that a husband should support his wife.

Preparing for War

Europe had been preparing for war since 1938. Many people hoped it would not happen. The horrors and losses of World War One were too close. Some women had campaigned for peace between the wars. However, as war became inevitable women knew they would have to play their part. In fact, far more women would be involved in World War Two than in World War One.

A family tries out its gas masks. During World War Two, everybody in the UK had to carry a mask in case the Germans dropped bombs containing poison gas.

Votes for Women

Between 1918–39 Women in many countries gained the vote

1918 British women over 30 gain the vote; women over 21 can be Members of Parliament (MPs)

1918 Austrian, Hungarian, Latvian and Lithuanian women gain the vote

1919 German and Polish women gain the vote

1920 American, Czechoslovakian and Albanian women gain the vote

1928 British women over 21 have the right to vote on an equal basis with men

1932 Spanish and Thai women have the vote

1934 Brazilian and Cuban women have the vote

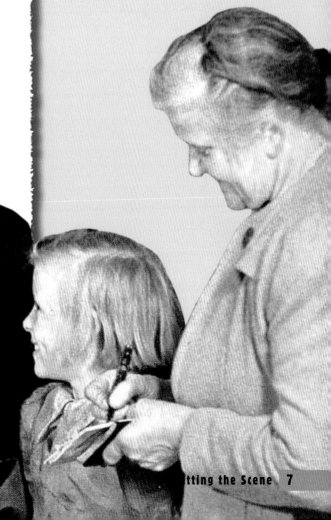

Volunteering to Help

On 3 September 1939, Britain and its empire declared war on Germany after German troops invaded Poland. World War Two had begun. In Britain thousands of women offered their help.

Women ambulance-service volunteers practise carrying stretchers in 1939. Their skills would soon be needed after the Luftwaffe *(German air force) began to bomb British cities.*

Women in Nazi Germany

German women had the vote but the National Socialist (Nazi) Party did not believe in women's rights. Women joined the Party and there was a Nazi Women's League. Girls and young women joined the Hitler Youth and the German Girls' League. They were told their main job was to be good wives and produce children. Women with large families were awarded a Cross of Motherhood.

Volunteers in every Field

British women volunteered to be nurses, ambulance drivers and air-raid wardens. Some joined the Auxiliary Territorial Army (ATS), which was formed in 1938. Many women, particularly older women or those with small children, could not do full-time work. Instead, they joined voluntary organisations.

Women's Voluntary Service (WVS)

The largest women's voluntary organisation was the Women's Voluntary Service (WVS). It was formed in 1938, with just five members. By 1941 the WVS had more than one million members throughout Britain, most of them middle-class women.

The WVS gave help wherever it was needed on the "Home Front". In September 1939, WVS women in distinctive grey-green uniforms helped evacuate children out of the cities, away from the risk of air raids. It was a huge job. More than one million children were evacuated in just three days.

Food, Clothing and Comfort

When air raids pulverised British cities the WVS worked with civil defence workers to care for bombed-out civilians. They set up mobile canteens, organised rest centres and found temporary housing for people whose homes had been destroyed. They distributed clothing parcels – Bundles for Britain – from Canada and the USA. The WVS also provided tea, snacks and cigarettes for thousands of soldiers. When they were not on call, the WVS, like women in all the warring countries, knitted countless balaclavas, scarves, gloves and socks for servicemen. In the USA, membership in the American Women's Voluntary Service (AWVS) grew as women volunteered for wartime relief work, helping the families of servicemen fighting abroad.

66 *...Nobody is more welcome to the "bombed-out", wardens and demolition workers than the WVS with their mobile canteens. Now there is a bite to eat and a cup of tea to hearten them. That's only one of the jobs WVS do, voluntarily ... and they nearly all have homes to run as well.* **99**

Text from 1944 advertisement aiming to recruit British women for the WVS.

An American Women's Voluntary Service (AWVS) relief worker helps a girl choose a dress from a clothing bank in 1944.

Calling all Women

Between 1939–45 millions of women entered the labour force. As men went off to fight, women replaced them as workers. Their contribution to the war effort was huge.

US artist Norman Rockwell's 1943 picture of factory worker "Rosie the Riveter" became one of the most famous images of World War Two.

THE SATURDAY EVENING

POST

MAY 29, 1943   10¢

BEGINNING—A NEW KELLAND SERIAL
Heart on Her Sleeve

EDGAR SNOW REPORTS ON GERMAN ATROCITIES

Opening doors

War work created new opportunities for women. In Britain and the United States married women entered the workforce in huge numbers, something that would have been unthinkable before the war. In the USA at least 400,000 black women worked in manufacturing for the first time. Before that they could only work as domestic servants or on the land.

A Slow Start

When war began, men were immediately called up for armed service. Women were needed – to produce food, weapons, warships, uniforms and the other necessities of war. British women volunteered but the government was slow to use them. Many women were told to stay at home or in the jobs they had unless they were particularly qualified. The Women's Freedom League complained bitterly that "the Government is not making anything like the full use of the Woman Power of the country."

Conscripting Women

By 1941 Britain desperately needed at least a million more workers. Government propaganda and radio broadcasts urged women to come into the factories and "do their bit". From December the government formally conscripted (called up) women. Britain was the first country ever to do this.

First, only single women aged 20–30 were called up. Later, all women aged 19–51 were conscripted. By 1943, nine out of ten single women and eight out of ten married women were in the forces, Land Army or war industries. The total number of British women in war work was about 7,750,000 – two million more than in 1939.

Around the World

The Soviet Union drafted millions of women into essential war work. Mobilisation of women was greater there than anywhere as women replaced the 20 million men who left to fight. In the USA, posters featuring Rosie the Riveter or Wanda the Welder helped to bring more than six million women into the workforce. In Australia, New Zealand, Canada and South Africa women were also recruited for wartime production. In Germany, however, women were not recruited until late in the war.

Types of Work

Women did every job imaginable – on railways, on the land, in transport and in factories. They worked as engineers, builders, welders, electricians and chemists. Many were doing jobs once thought only suitable for men.

Canadian First

Some Canadian women worked on assembly lines producing military aircraft. Elsie MacGill (1905–80) supervised one of the assembly plants. She was the first Canadian woman to graduate as an electrical engineer and the world's first female aeronautical designer. Her staff produced about 1,450 Hawker Hurricane fighter aircraft. Some were used in the Battle of Britain (Aug–Oct 1940).

Thousands of women worked in munitions factories during the war. These women workers are making huge bombs to be dropped from aircraft.

Hard-working Women

Recruitment posters showed factory work as glamorous and desirable. The reality was different. Women worked long hours in difficult conditions. Many looked after a home, too.

This picture, Ruby Loftus screwing a Breech-ring, *was painted by Dame Laura Knight in 1943. It shows gun factory worker Ruby Loftus performing a task that required great precision. Male colleagues were amazed that a woman could do this better than they.*

For and Against

Wartime production of weapons, tanks, aircraft, warships, submarines, parachutes and uniforms would not have been possible without women. However, not everyone wanted women to work. Prime Minister Winston Churchill thought it would damage family life. One man said: "home life would vanish" and "men will come back to cold and untidy homes, with no meal ready". Male trade unionists and workers saw women as a threat to their wages and a man's role as head of the family. Most women, however, wanted to work.

Working Conditions

Women without families – usually young, single women – could be sent anywhere they were needed. They lived in hostels. Those with families worked nearer to home.

> **She's the girl**
> **That makes the thing**
> **That drills the hole**
> **That holds the spring**
> **That drives the rod**
> **That turns the knob**
> **That works the**
> **   thingumabob...**
> **That's going to win**
> **   the war**
>
> *World War Two popular song*

Factory women worked 60 or more hours a week with only short breaks for lunch and tea. Some had only one weekend off in three. Women complained that factory work was boring and repetitive. The noise of machines was deafening and women worked in dirty, dangerous conditions, sometimes without ventilation or light because of the blackout. There were often no lavatories for women. Women who had worked before the war knew what to expect but new workers were often shocked. Munitions workers had to use explosive and toxic materials. Some lost fingers or hands if there was an accident. Air raids added to the danger. Women often had to keep working until the last minute before diving for shelter.

A Double Burden

After a long day's work, women with families had to go home to cook and clean. They needed to shop, which meant queuing. As war progressed, some employers set up nurseries and crèches and introduced flexible working hours. Lavatories and washrooms were also installed.

Skills and Pay

During the war women earned more than ever before, particularly in skilled work on the railways, in shipbuilding, aircraft production and engineering. Even so, they earned less than men, sometimes as low as half a man's wage for the same work. There were complaints and in 1943, skilled women workers who were earning less than male cleaners went on strike in Glasgow, Scotland. But actions like this were rare.

Dressing the part

War work had a big impact on women's clothes. A factory was no place for fashion. Women donned bibs and braces, dungarees and trousers to keep clean. For safety, they covered their hair in bandanas or scarves made into turbans, something that became a key wartime image.

"*A bomb hit the factory before we were given permission to go to the shelter. The paint department went up. I saw several people flying through the air and I just ran home. I was suffering from shock.*"

Muriel Simkin, munitions worker

On the Land

Many women worked on the land. It was hard, backbreaking work. Most had never done farm work before but their efforts kept food supplies flowing.

Women's Land Army

In 1939 the Women's Land Army (WLA) was formed. It had existed in World War One but was disbanded in 1919. Now, as men left farms to fight, it was needed again. By 1944, some 90,000 women had joined. Most were young. They were known as Land Girls. Women in Australia, Canada, the USA and the Soviet Union also did essential work on the land.

A recruiting poster urges British women to help farmers by joining the Women's Land Army.

Real-life recruitment

Recruitment posters usually showed romanticised pictures of land workers. They never looked quite real. One poster did feature a real Land Girl. Her name was Mary Feddon. During her training someone photographed her with a newborn calf. She could not find the negative. To her surprise, she later saw her picture on a Land Army recruitment poster.

Work, Pay and Conditions

Many young women came from cities and towns. They had been office or shop workers, hairdressers or in other jobs that had nothing to do with farming. Some were conscientious objectors. They were given a medical check-up, perhaps some training, then sent to work in the countryside. They lived in hostels or on farms. Some stayed in old workers' cottages without running water, gas or electricity.

Land Girls worked 50-hour weeks for very little pay. They drove tractors, planted and harvested, spread muck and dug ditches. They looked after cattle and poultry and did the milking. They even caught rats to prevent them destroying crops.

Girls worked from early morning to nightfall. They had Sundays off and a home visit once every six months. Many complained about the food.

At first male farmers thought women would not manage heavy work on the land. They were wrong. By 1943 Land Girls were helping to produce 70 per cent of Britain's food.

Lumberjills

About 6,000 women joined the Timber Corps. They were nicknamed "Lumberjills". They did heavy forestry work, felling trees, cutting poles for mineshafts, loading charcoal and making wooden roads. Land Girls and Lumberjills sometimes worked with Italian prisoners of war (POWs), who were put to work on the land.

In most of the warring countries, women helped with a range of farming work.

" We were quite a happy crowd ... The food was the worst thing ... the way it was cooked ... The rice was so hard it was like chicken feed, the potatoes were cooked with the dirt still on them ... we only had three sandwiches to last a full day in the woods. **"**

Annice Gibbs, Timber Corps

Women in the Forces

Women were not allowed to fight but they joined women's sections in all the armed forces: army, navy and air force.

Charity Adams-Earley

Charity Adams-Earley was the first black American woman to serve as a commissioned officer in the Women's Army Corps. Segregation (separation) of blacks and whites still existed in the USA and few black American women were allowed to join the US forces. Despite prejudice, she became a major and commanded the first unit of black WACs to serve in France.

Knickers or jumpers

Women in the WRNS were known as Wrens. They wore blue serge uniforms. Their knickers were navy blue too. Some Wrens found a good use for them. "We used to turn the knickers upside down, sew across for shoulder seams, take out the gusset and make them into jumpers."

Women's Services

British women joined the Auxiliary Territorial Service (ATS), the women's section of the army, the Women's Royal Naval Service (WRNS) or the Women's Auxiliary Air Force (WAAF). There was also the Women's Transport Service. By 1943 more than 500,000 women were serving in the ATS, WRNS and WAAF combined.

American women served in the Women's Army Corps (WAC), and were sent to all theatres of war. They joined the women's section of the navy, which was known as WAVES – Women Accepted for Voluntary Service – as well as the marines and coastguards. Canadian and Australian women also served in their armed forces. The shortage of manpower in Germany meant that German women, too, were enlisted into the forces.

Lined up for inspection: women of the WAAF on parade in 1943.

Non-combat Duties

Women were not allowed to fight but they wore uniforms and learned to drill and take orders just like men. They worked as drivers, cooks and clerks, freeing men to fight. As war progressed, they did more. In Britain the WAAFs and WRNS worked in command centres and operation rooms as telephone operators or using radar and wireless to plot the movement of ships and planes. Sometimes operation rooms were bombed but the women kept on working. Occasionally, they had the horrible experience of hearing pilots screaming as their planes went down in flames.

Anti-aircraft Guns

Women worked alongside men on anti-aircraft guns, known in Britain as ack-ack. It was heavy, dangerous work. Women moved the searchlights to light up incoming planes so they could be shot down, which made them targets as well. They positioned the guns but were not allowed to fire them. The WRNS were not allowed on fighting ships but operated heavy launches and overhauled depth charges and torpedoes.

British women served in France, Egypt and Asia. In 1940, ATS telephonists were among the last to be evacuated from Dunkirk.

Fighting Women

Some women did fight. Russian women fought on the front in artillery and tank units. Some were snipers. Uniformed Polish women fought against invading German troops and an all-woman Indian regiment called the Rani fought in Burma. In Germany, women's fighting battalions were created towards the end of the war.

MILITARY WOMEN

Britain
Some 500,000 enlisted in the services during the war. In 1943, more than 56,000 were in anti-aircraft command.
Women in the services in 1943 were:
- WRNS 180,000
- WAAF 180,000
- ATS 210,000

Canada
More than 45,000 volunteered for military service.

Australia
About 78,000 joined war services.

USA
Nearly 400,000 women served in the US military, including 800 Native Americans.
Summer 1943 figures were:
- WACs 100,000
- WAVES 92,000
- Marines 20,000
- Coastguards (SPARS) 11,000
- WASPs (Women's airforce) 1,000
- Army Nurse Corps 57,000
- Navy Nurse Corps 11,000

Soviet Union
About 800,000 served in the Red Army. 300,000 belonged to anti-aircraft units.

Germany
450,000 joined auxiliary services. 65,000 – 100,000 served in anti-aircraft units.

Airborne Women

Most women who joined the air force worked on the ground at airfields or in communications centres. Some women flew and ferried planes. Soviet women fought in the skies.

Flying Heroine

In 1940 the *Girl's Own Paper*, a British comic for girls, featured an exciting new heroine – Worrals of the WAAF. Her adventures appeared throughout the war. Unlike a real WAAF member, Worrals flew fighter planes as well as transport. She even shot down an enemy aircraft. Worrals possibly helped recruit a lot of young women into the WAAF.

Pilots of the WAAF.

Joining the Air Force

By 1943 some 180,000 British women had joined the Women's Auxiliary Air Force (WAAF). Thousands of Canadian women joined the Women's Division of the Royal Canadian Air Force when it was formed in 1941. In 1943 more than 1,000 women joined the elite Women's Air Service Pilots (WASPs). German women joined the Luftwaffe.

Women were not allowed to fly combat missions. Most worked on the ground, providing support for male fighter pilots. Some worked as electricians and mechanics. Others worked in aerial photography units and as "plotters", working in new radar stations tracking incoming bombers. Women packed parachutes and developed navigation skills. WAAFs staffed barrage balloons.

Flying Role

There were skilled women pilots. They could not take part in combat but they flew planes from factories to airfields and squadrons wherever they were needed. In Britain, the Air Transport Auxiliary (ATA) was formed in 1939 to do this work. Nearly half the ATA pilots were women. They included famous British pilot Amy Johnson. Canadian and American women also flew with the ATA including the American aviator, Jackie Cochran, who later formed the WASPs.

Women flew all sorts of planes, including Spitfires, Hurricanes and large bombers. They were not always welcome. The male editor of the flying magazine *Aeroplane* said women pilots were a "menace". In fact ATA women had far fewer crashes than men.

In the USA more than 900 WASPs ferried over 12,000 aircraft from factories to airfields. They towed gliders and targets and flew practice missions to train bomber crews. Like their British counterparts, WASPs were discriminated against. They remained civilians and their role was not formally recognised until 1977.

Night Witches

The Soviet Union was the first country to allow women to fly combat missions. In 1941, Russian pilot Marina Raskova created three all-women air combat squadrons: a fighter squadron, a short-range dive-bomber squadron and a night fighter-bomber squadron. The night fighters became known as the "Night Witches". In ramshackle biplanes, the Night Witches flew 24,000 night bombing raids over German front lines, targeting railways, ammunition dumps and artillery positions.

Decorated for Bravery

In May 1940 Joan Daphne Mary Pearson became the first WAAF to be decorated for outstanding bravery. She was awarded the George Cross for pulling an RAF pilot from a burning plane and using her body to shield him from a 55-kg bomb that exploded nearby. She survived and saved his life.

A woman pilot prepares to take off and deliver a much-needed aircraft to a front-line squadron.

Nurses

Women had nursed the wounded in World War One. Now nurses were needed for World War Two. Many served on the front lines.

Military and Civilian

Thousands of women in the warring nations came forward as nurses. Some were part of the military, attached mainly to the army but also with the air force and navy. They were subject to military rules and discipline.

There were also civilian nurses – professional or volunteers. British women worked with the Red Cross, the Voluntary Aid Detachment (VAD) or other non-military groups.

Nurses on all the warring sides often worked in appalling and dangerous conditions.

> **There were stretchers all down the middle of the tent, there were charred bodies everywhere, some were quiet and dying, others screaming with pain, all with severe burns.**
>
> *Iris Ogilvia, Canadian nurse*

On the Front Line

Nurses worked at home and abroad. In Britain, nurses on the home front worked in general hospitals, special units treating facial or other injuries, and first-aid centres. They treated air raid victims and wounded soldiers back from the front.

In World War One, nurses were not supposed to work near the front line, although many did. In World War Two, it was policy to send nurses as close to the front line as possible. As a result, they were exposed to more dangers than almost any other women in the war. During Dunkirk, 1,300 British nurses dressed the wounded in the open while the beaches were bombed.

Nurses went to war zones in Europe, North Africa and the Far East. Some worked in field or evacuation hospitals. These were mobile units where nurses gave emergency treatment to the wounded straight off the battlefield. They became skilled at packing up and moving supplies and patients if enemy troops broke through. Nurses also worked in hospitals, which were situated further back from the front line. These were often bombed or abandoned hospitals or schools. They nursed soldiers on hospital trains and ships, and on planes.

Harsh Conditions

Nurses learned to survive and cope in harsh, extremely dangerous and distressing conditions. They worked long hours treating terrible wounds and diseases like typhus, malaria and diptheria. They improvised when supplies ran low, re-using bandages or turning trousers into stretchers. Some nurses gave their own blood for transfusions. Hospitals and hospital ships were bombed and nurses were killed. Many allied nurses were taken prisoner by the Japanese and suffered dreadful mistreatment. Some nurses treated survivors of the concentration camps. They were shocked to learn that German nurses had assisted in the Holocaust.

A Nurse's Story

Olwen "Bobbie" Roberts of Southport, Lancashire, joined the Red Cross and was called up in 1940. She was put onto a surgical ward nursing soldiers arriving from Dunkirk. These were "incredibly bad, extensive burns, a lot of amputations". Later, she was sent to York Military Hospital. Air raids were vicious but nurses had to work through. However, there were amusing moments. "During an air raid, we were expected to put spare mattresses over the men who were bedridden and fill the baths with water.... I was on my own... I couldn't do it, I was laughing so much and so were the men."

Olwen later joined the VAD. In 1944 she was sent to India to nurse. She travelled by sea in a huge convoy as one of 200 VADs. She was sent to a military hospital in Chittagong, Bengal where she nursed seriously wounded British and Indian soldiers and gained a reputation for being able to sniff out gangrene. She lived in a bamboo hut called a basha. The work was hard but on time off, "you went to one party or another". In 1946 she returned to England. Of her wartime nursing she says: "I am immensely pleased to have taken part. It was a very important part of my life."

Making Do

Food and clothing were rationed during the war. As war continued, the shortages got worse. Women had to find inventive ways of making do.

Wartime Needs

Women in Britain, France and Germany were most affected by shortages. Even so, women in the USA, New Zealand, Australia and Canada were also urged to make do and mend because their countries' resources were needed for war.

The Kitchen Front

When it came to food, government propaganda was aimed directly at women. The Ministry of Food coined the phrase "kitchen front" to describe women's efforts in the kitchen. The BBC broadcast "kitchen-front advice". To women who were juggling work, home, children and limited rations, each day must have felt like a battle in itself.

Rationing

Britain introduced food rationing in January 1940. Butter, bacon and ham were the first to be rationed. By 1942, sugar, tea, jam, milk, cheese, eggs and cooking oil were also rationed. As German submarines sank more and more Allied ships, imported fruit such as bananas disappeared completely.

As persons often solely responsible for running the home, women had to produce wholesome, nourishing meals with dried eggs and milk, home-grown fruit and vegetables, and limited amounts of meat and fish. A Ministry of Food was set up and bombarded women with advice on how to cook with wartime rations. Radio programmes, leaflets and cookbooks advised women to use carrots or apples for sweeteners and recommended dishes like bread pudding or lentil sausages – sausage-shaped items that had no meat in them at all. Restrictions pushed British women's resources to the limit but, in fact, the wartime diet was quite healthy.

Waste not, Want not

From 1941 clothes were rationed or at least put on a points system. Each person had a certain number of points; different clothes had different point values. Instead of buying new clothes, women mended and re-used. They unpicked old woollen clothes and re-used the wool to make socks, balaclavas and anything else they could think of. Knitting became a national pastime as women knitted in air-raid shelters, at work and anywhere they could find time.

Women made skirts from men's trousers, created a jumper by adding knitted sleeves to a waistcoat or made a blouse from dusters. Nothing was thrown away or wasted. The WVS set up clothes exchanges while government propaganda urged women to "make do and mend". In Germany, where women experienced severe shortages from 1941, women darned clothes with dyed string when cotton thread ran out.

Beetroot and Tea

Make-up became scarce. Instead of lipstick, women used beetroot juice to stain their lips. There were no stockings, so women went bare legged or stained their legs with cold tea or gravy browning. Stockings had seams up the back of the leg, so women drew seams onto the back of their legs with an eyebrow pencil.

Making jam

The Women's Institute (WI), a long-established women's voluntary organisation, was famous for making jam and preserves. In 1941 they made more than 2,000 tonnes of preserves from home-grown fruit. The WI also harvested rosehips, which were made into a vitamin-rich syrup for children.

Queuing in all kinds of weather to buy food for their families was a common wartime experience for millions of women.

Behind the Scenes

Women worked behind the scenes as code-breakers or with highly secret information. Others were secret agents or resistance fighters.

Noor Inayat Khan

Noor Inayat Khan, a descendant of Tipu Sultan, a Muslim ruler of India, was born in the Soviet Union. Her family settled in France. When Germany invaded France, she escaped to England and worked with the Red Cross, then the WAAF. She became a special agent, nicknamed Madeleine, and was flown to France in 1943.

She joined an underground network as a wireless operator and kept working even when members of the network were caught. Ultimately the Gestapo arrested and interrogated her and sent her to Dachau concentration camp. There she and three other women agents – Yolande Beekmann, Elaine Plewman and Madeleine Damerment – were murdered by the SS.

Breaking the Code

Women were involved in top-secret work. About 2,000 women worked at Bletchley Park, the British Government's Code and Cipher School. Using what was called the "Enigma" machine, which was a type of early computer, they learned to decode messages coming in from Germany. Women telephonists and secretaries were among the staff at the Cabinet War Office in London. No one could talk about the work they were doing.

Special Operations

By 1940 Germany had occupied France. The British government set up what was known as Special Operations Executive (SOE) to send secret agents into France to help the French underground resistance. Women were recruited to help. Many came from the First Aid Nursing Yeomanry (FANY), an elite women's organisation first created in 1907. At first they were code-breakers and created forged documents that could be used in occupied Europe. From 1942 they were sent into occupied territories as secret agents. In all, the SOE sent 470 agents into France, 39 of whom were women.

It was extremely dangerous work. Agents were trained, given false names and identities and parachuted into occupied territories to make contact with the underground. Many carried wireless transmitters. If captured by the Gestapo, they faced torture and execution.

An estimated 200 agents lost their lives; 15 of them were women. They included Noor Inayat Khan (see box), Odette Sansom, Violette Szabo and Yvonne Rudelat.

Resistance Fighters

Women throughout occupied Europe joined resistance movements and partisan groups to fight against the Germans. They included Jewish women such as Vitka Kempner and Ruzka Korezak and Frenchwomen such as Elaine Mordeaux, a top French resistance commander, who led a unit of 200 fighters. She and her unit held up a German tank advance during the D-Day offensive.

Yugoslavian and Hungarian women fought in partisan groups, the first all-woman Yugoslav partisan group being formed in 1942. Some German and Italian women also resisted Nazi control. They included Wilma Lauterwasse-Pflugfelder, who worked with the underground resistance.

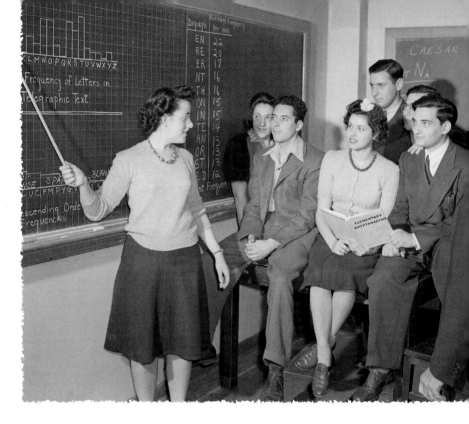

Women played a key role in efforts to break enemy codes. Here, a female lecturer instructs a class at Brooklyn College, New York, on code-breaking techniques, 1942.

❝ I followed the war wherever I could reach it.❞

Martha Gellhorn, US foreign correspondent who reported from Finland, Hong Kong, Burma, Singapore and Britain.

Recording the war

Women journalists, photographers and artists recorded the war in newspapers, magazines, on radio and in paintings. Some worked on the front line under fire, before filing their stories to newspapers back home. Sonia Tomara of the *New York Herald Tribune* flew on bombing raids and Margaret Bourke-White of *Life* magazine was torpedoed. Margaret Higgins reported on the concentration camp at Buchenwald. In Britain, Dame Laura Knight worked as an official war artist.

Getting Through

Despite the hardships of war, women managed to enjoy themselves. There were dances, music, humour and friendships. Professional entertainers boosted morale at home and abroad.

" We never stopped singing. We knew all the words... We could lose ourselves... forget the horrors of war. "

Mickie Hulton Storie, ATS

Lilli Marlene

The most popular song of World War Two had a woman's name – Lilli Marlene (Lili Marleen in German). It was based on a love poem written by a German soldier in 1917 and popularised by a Swedish cabaret singer, Lale Andersen. With its haunting words and melody, the song was a favourite with German troops, particularly the Afrika Korps. The British 8th Army heard and adapted the song, which was recorded in English by Anne Shelton. It became equally popular among the Allies.

A Difficult Time

Women's lives were stressful, as war disrupted all aspects of daily life. Work, air raids, food and clothing shortages, keeping a home going and anxiety about male relatives took their toll. No one knew what the next day would bring. Among the Allies, British women had a long and difficult war.

Despite all this, women still found time to have fun. After the war, many women commented on the close friendships they had made with other women and how people helped each other through difficulties. Jokes – about war, bombs and wartime food – were part of everyday life.

Music and Dancing

Popular music helped to lift morale. Women factory workers in Britain listened to the BBC's *Music While You Work*, which played constantly in factories, even if the noise of machinery sometimes drowned out the sound. In the USA, factories introduced piped music for women workers, who sang along to heart-throb crooners like Bing Crosby.

After work, women went dancing, sometimes to well-known swing or jazz bands. When American soldiers, known as GIs, arrived in Britain, they introduced a new dance craze – the jitterbug. Young women learned eagerly, often dancing with American soldiers, sometimes to the disgust of British men. Thousands of American soldiers took British brides back to the USA after the war.

Women entertainers such as Ivy Benson toured the world doing shows for servicemen.

Entertaining the Troops

Women entertainers boosted morale with live concerts for troops at home and overseas. The British had the Entertainments National Services Association. It was known as ENSA or, for a joke, as Every Night Something Awful. Popular ENSA performers included Gracie Fields, known as "Our Gracie", Anne Shelton, the "force's favourite" and Vera Lynn, the "force's sweetheart". They gave thousands of live performances. Vera Lynn singing "White Cliffs of Dover" became a wartime classic. American entertainers, such as the Andrews Sisters, and superstar Marlene Dietrich toured overseas troop bases and hospitals bringing a taste of home to battle-weary soldiers.

Living for now

Teenagers and young women had more freedom during the war than ever before. They went out on their own or with groups of friends, living life for the moment and having fun when they could. The future was uncertain and there were many brief love affairs between young women and soldiers.

After the War

The war ended in 1945. Women were exhausted, and many longed for a return to normality. But war had changed women's lives.

Women's Voices

Women's own voices tell us a lot about World War Two. Women kept diaries, or wrote letters that give a glimpse of what war was actually like for them at the time. Some women kept diaries for a British study called "Mass Observation". These are stored at Sussex University. Since the war ended, people have recorded women's memories of war as oral history. All these provide valuable insights into women's wartime experiences.

Back into the Home

Some historians believe the Allies would not have won the war without women's contribution. Millions of women had played an essential role. When the war ended, it seemed as if women were no longer needed. Wartime propaganda had urged women to play their part. Now women were told it was their patriotic duty to give up their jobs to men. Images of the "ideal" family showed women in the kitchen, not the factory.

As factories went back to peacetime production, women were laid off or moved back into lower-paid traditional women's jobs. Women welders went back to being typists. One million British women left the workforce. In the United States, three million women came out of work. Some women were pleased to stop.

Joy at the end of the war led to parties in all the victorious countries. Here, women in Lancashire dance at a street party in May 1945. But how much had the war really changed their lives?

Others resented giving up their jobs. Widows, whose husbands had been killed, worried about how to support their families.

Independence and Welfare

To start with many women wanted to be housewives again and it looked as if pre-war traditions of women being dependent on men would return. In the long run they did not. Divorce soared after the war. In 1945 there were twice as many divorces as in 1939. Married women had worked, run homes and brought up children single-handedly while their husbands were away. Husbands and wives could not always adjust when peace returned.

Social changes helped women. In 1945 British women received child benefit for the first time, which gave them some financial independence. The Welfare State was introduced, which provided benefits such as free health care.

Even after women had been laid off from work in 1945, there were still more women in the labour force than in 1939 and, after a short break, this trend continued. From the 1950s increasing numbers of women, including married women, were entering the labour force.

Equal Rights

During the war women had gained confidence and a sense of their own value. They had proved they were just as capable as men. In the USA, black women had proved they were as able as white women. Women's place in society had changed, even if it was not obvious in 1945. By the 1960s, women worldwide were campaigning for, and demanding equal rights.

❝ During the war we did everything a man could do except fight, and after it was over there was a lot of unrest as well as happiness and sadness, all mixed in together. ❞

Canadian woman, RCAF

Helen Bamber

Helen Bamber was born in London in 1925 to Polish-Jewish parents. In 1945, as the youngest member of UNRRA (United Nations Relief and Rehabilitation Administration), she went into Belsen concentration camp shortly after it was liberated. In 1985 she established the Medical Foundation for the Care of Victims of Torture. Of the war, she says: "I can speak of the fun we had... I remember laughing and joking during the bombing of London. What I don't like to remember is the fear I had then and the fear I have now that it could all happen again."

Glossary

Allies Britain, the Commonwealth and other countries who fought together against Nazi Germany. Germany, Italy and Japan were known as the Axis powers.

Anti-aircraft guns Guns used to shoot down aircraft. Also known as ack-ack.

Auxiliary Someone who provides a supporting role. For example, the Auxiliary Territorial Service (ATS) provided support so that men could go and fight.

Balaclava Covering for the head or neck that leaves only part of the face exposed.

Barrage balloons Huge, hydrogen-filled balloons that floated above cities to protect them from low-flying enemy aeroplanes. If an aircraft flew too low it would snag in a balloon's cable and crash.

Billeted Being housed in another person's home or in a hostel.

Blackout Switching off all lights at night so that enemy aircraft would not be able to see houses or factories.

British Empire Countries colonised by Britain. By 1939 the Empire still included Canada, Australia, New Zealand, South Africa and India. They fought with Britain during World War Two.

Civilian A woman or man who is an ordinary citizen rather than a member of the armed forces.

Civil defence People, often volunteers, whose work was to defend civilians on the home front.

Conscientious objector A person who, for reasons of conscience, will not fight or join the military.

Conscription Being called up for military service or work.

D-Day 6 June 1944. The day on which Allied forces invaded Nazi-occupied France.

Evacuation Movement of large groups of people from a dangerous place to one of safety.

Gangrene The death and decay of body tissue that sets in when blood flow to the area is interrupted.

Gestapo *Geheimnis Staatspolizei* – the Nazi secret police force.

GI An American soldier. GI stands for Government Issue. American soldiers received GI trousers, GI shirts and various other GI items. In time, they began to call themselves GIs.

Holocaust Term given to the mass murder of Jews by the Nazis during World War Two.

Home front A term that describes how war affected civilians' daily lives. People sometimes said civilians fought on the home front, just as soldiers fought on the front line.

Munitions Weapons.

Nazi party Adolf Hitler's National Socialist (Nazi) Party.

Propaganda Information put out in radio broadcasts, leaflets and posters by governments or organisations to change minds or influence what people do.

Radar A method of detecting distant objects, like aircraft and ships, and finding their positions. Stands for "radio detection and ranging".

Rationing A fixed allowance of food, provisions, fuel and so on, especially in time of scarcity, such as war, set by the government.

Soviet Union The world's first communist state. It existed from 1917–91 and included what is now called Russia. It was also known as the USSR (Union of Soviet Socialist Republics).

Volunteer Someone who chooses to do something rather than being conscripted or called up.

WEBSITES

www.spartacus.schoolnet.co.uk/2WW.htm
A comprehensive site covering every aspect of World War Two, including both the military campaigns and the home front.

www.bbc.co.uk/history/war/wwtwo/index.shtml
The official BBC site on the war, with numerous photographs, maps and spoken word extracts.

www.historyplace.com/worldwar2/timeline/ww2time.htm
A detailed timeline of events from 1918 to the end of World War Two, with many photographs.

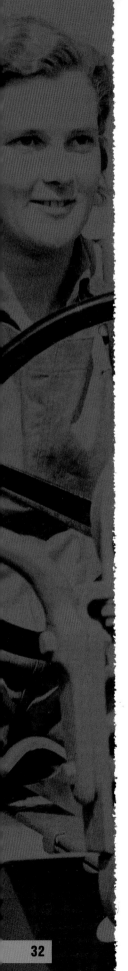

Index